Christmas 1997

# *Traditional* Quilting

# *Traditional* Quilting

## Isabel Stanley and Jenny Watson

HERMES HOUSE

This edition first published in 1997 by Hermes House

© Anness Publishing Limited 1997

Hermes House is an imprint of Anness Publishing Limited
Hermes House
88–89 Blackfriars Road
London SE1 8HA

ISBN 1 901289 86 9

Publisher: Joanna Lorenz
Project Editor: Judith Simons
Assistant Editor: Daniel King
Text Editor: Judy Walker
Photographer: Gloria Nicol
Step Photographer: Lucy Tizard
Designer: Louise Morley
Illustrator: Lucinda Ganderton

A CIP catalogue record for this book is available from the British Library.

Printed and bound in Hong Kong

1 3 5 7 9 10 8 6 4 2

# CONTENTS

· · · · · ·

# INTRODUCTION

Patchwork, quilting and appliqué have developed over the centuries in many different countries. Techniques have crossed continents, fallen in and out of fashion, and evolved according to cultural and economic changes.

Originally these crafts were practised through necessity, rather than pleasure. Patchwork was an economic way of using scraps for those who could not afford new fabric; appliqué was used to replace worn areas on a textile; and quilting provided vital warmth. However, many historic examples show that both professional and domestic makers combined function with decoration. Patchwork developed intricate patterns known as mosaic patchwork, made of hundreds of tiny geometric shapes pieced together. This was a time-consuming method of construction, with traditional hand-sewn pieces of cloth backed with paper. Closer examination of these papers reveals part of the makers' lives as templates were often cut from old letters, newspapers or magazines. It is sometimes possible to date the pieces, or to show that a quilt had proved to be too ambitious for the original maker, only to be unearthed years later and completed by another member of the family.

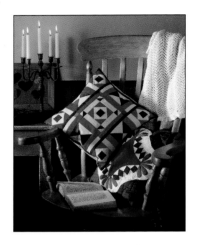

*ABOVE: This design is based on a sampler quilt made in Pennsylvania, in about 1870.*

*BELOW: A late 19th-century Welsh quilt.*

People often re-used fabric scraps which were simply too valuable to throw away. In the Victorian era, a fashion emerged for using rich and opulent fabrics in the randomly arranged crazy patchwork, in contrast to patchwork's humble and utilitarian beginnings. Patchwork also became a vehicle for practising stitches, and a way to express personal messages and sentimental phrases. Work was embellished with elaborate embroidery stitches and motifs, ribbons and buttons, so that the whole textile was imbued with memories. These amazingly decorative quilts provided a canvas on which a needlewoman could display her skills.

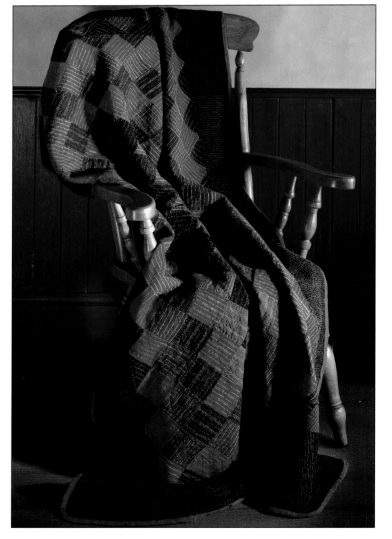

Quilts have always been associated with the celebration of important events. Typically they would be made to mark a particular occasion, with the nature of the celebration reflected in the choice of design or quilting. The Double Wedding Ring patchwork design, for example, was worked to mark a marriage or wedding anniversary and was made from interlinking rings, each constructed from tiny patches. It would be inadvisable to attempt an entire quilt with this motif today, because it is so time consuming. Appearances are deceptive, however. The Cathedral Window patchwork design, which looks complicated, is in fact relatively easy to construct and is more an exercise in fabric origami as the patches consist of folded and re-folded cloth.

In the early stages of its history, quilting was considered simply as a utilitarian technique. Two layers of fabric were placed either side of a filling of wadding (batting). The three layers were then stitched together to create a flexible and insulating textile. Although these basic skills fulfilled the practical necessity of providing a warm bedcover, people quickly recognized the decorative potential of quilting to create interesting relief patterns. Trapunto, or stuffed, quilting and corded, or Italian, quilting are two such techniques, which were not used for their insulating qualities but became popular for embellishing clothing. In corded quilting, two layers of fabric are placed together on top of a loosely woven underpiece and a pattern of narrow channels are stitched. Cord is then threaded through from the wrong side to create relief pattern. This method is often used in conjunction with traditional quilting to outline a motif, or to delineate an area. Trapunto quilting is constructed in much the same way, but instead of channels shapes are stitched and filled with wadding from the wrong side. Shadow quilting, another historic technique, uses a sheer fabric as a top layer over coloured wool or cord to create subtle areas of diffused colour. Traditionally made in white fabrics, it can also be effective in other colours.

Appliqué originated in the early spirit of "make do and mend", and developed along decorative and creative lines. The technique of broderie perse was practised during the 18th and 19th centuries to preserve favourite motifs from imported Indian cotton chintzes. These offered a strong contrast to Western fabrics, featuring bold, brilliant designs with large birds, cornucopias and flowers. Such was their popularity that British manufacturers suffered a loss of trade and a law was passed first to limit their importation and finally to ban their use. Unable to replenish their stocks, needlewomen cut out the motifs to appliqué on to other fabrics.

Inspired by historical examples of patchwork, quilting and appliqué, these step-by-step projects are guaranteed to give pleasure to the maker. They have been devised to encourage the amateur needleworker to attempt traditional methods, and although challenging, the projects are not so large or complex as to discourage the beginner. It is advisable to start small and simple – projects such as lavender bags, nightdress cases and bootees are ideal for beginners. To help re-create the romance of the past, choose evocative fabrics, such as velvets, satins, taffetas and brocades. Do not forget trimmings, search out unusual beads, ribbons, fringing and tassels to add to your collection.

# BASIC TECHNIQUES
• • • • • •

The many varied projects in this book feature a wealth of design ideas employing a wide range of techniques, both old and modern, and from all four corners of the world. You will discover the secrets of stained glass appliqué, string patchwork and corded quilting, along with shadow work, broderie perse and much more. However, there are many standard quilting, patchwork and appliqué techniques that need to be grasped before you begin a project – you will be coming across the same methods again and again.

## PATCHWORK TECHNIQUES

Pieced patchwork is made from fabric scraps that are cut into regular shapes and then sewn together in geometric patterns to form a mosaic of cloth. The patches can be pieced or joined together by one of two basic methods: by machine or by hand. Machining is quickest, but hand sewing gives a traditional look to a finished piece with slightly irregular seams. For the beginner, working over backing papers is the best way to make precise angled shapes when piecing by hand. Whichever method is chosen, accurate templates, meticulous measuring and cutting, careful stitching and thorough pressing are all vital for a professional finish.

### TEMPLATES

Accurate templates will allow you to make patches identical in size and shape that will fit perfectly together. There are several different types of template you can make or buy. You can cut them yourself from card (cardboard) or from firm, clear plastic (acetate). Alternatively, you can make window templates, which allow you to view the fabric. Always make a new template for each shape required in a project – old templates eventually become a little distorted round the edges. Templates can also be purchased ready-made in various shapes and sizes.

Patchwork templates should always include a seam allowance; in this book the seam allowance is usually 5 mm (¼ in). If you are using backing papers, you will need to cut two templates if using card or plastic – one with the seam allowance included for marking the fabric and one without the seam allowance for the backing paper. If using a window template, the outside edge of the frame is used to mark the fabric and the inside edge of the frame the backing paper.

### MAKING CARD (CARDBOARD) TEMPLATES

<u>1</u>

Transfer the design on to squared paper and cut round each shape with a sharp pair of scissors.

<u>2</u>

Glue the shapes to a piece of thin card (cardboard), and draw a seam allowance round each. Cut out the card.

<u>3</u>

Protect the seam allowance area with a thin coat of clear nail varnish.

## MAKING PLASTIC (ACETATE) TEMPLATES

Place the clear plastic (acetate) over the design and draw round each shape. Then draw a seam allowance round each and cut out. Being transparent, the template can be accurately positioned on the fabric.

## MAKING WINDOW TEMPLATES

Trace the shape on to card (cardboard), then draw a 5 mm (¼ in) seam allowance round it. Cut out the outer and inner parts, leaving a card frame the exact width of the seam allowance.

## MAKING CURVED TEMPLATES

For curved blocks, mark notches on the seam lines of the pattern before cutting it into sections. Cut out each template and then carefully cut out the notches with a craft knife.

# PREPARING PATCHES

Position the template on the fabric, lining up one straight edge with the grain of the fabric. Draw round it on to the reverse of the fabric using a vanishing marker, tailor's chalk or a soft pencil. Butt the shapes together to ensure a good fit.

## CUTTING OUT PATCHES IN GROUPS

### 1

Several patches can be cut at once using this method. Fold the fabric like a concertina and then staple the card (cardboard) template to the layers.

### 2

Use a sharp rotary cutter or a craft knife and press hard into the cutting mat.

### 3

Organize the cut pieces by stringing them on a length of thread. You can store them like this and remove them one at a time.

## ATTACHING BACKING PAPERS

Pin the backing papers to the reverse of the fabric patches. Fold over or press the seam allowance. Leaving a short free end of thread, tack (baste) along the middle of the seam allowance to the end of the side and trim the corners. Fold over the adjacent seam allowance and continue to tack. Repeat on all sides, leaving the thread ends free so that the threads and the backing papers can be removed easily once the work has been pieced.

## BACKING WITH INTERFACING

Iron-on interfacing can be used instead of backing papers. It is especially useful when machine piecing. Mark the patches on the interfacing adjacent to one another. Cut along the main lines first and then cut out the individual blocks. Iron these on to the reverse of the fabric, then mark a seam allowance round the interfacing on the fabric. Cut out the patches individually with scissors or as a group with a rotary cutter.

## PIECING OR JOINING PATCHES

Lay out the cut patches to work out the final arrangement. When you are happy with the design, you can begin piecing the patches. There are several different methods of doing this, depending on whether you are piecing by hand or using a sewing machine.

### HAND PIECING

Right sides facing, pin the prepared patches together. First pin each corner, and then pin at equidistant points along the side. Join the patches with a small, neat whip stitch – or overstitch – as shown. Insert the needle in one corner and work across to the other, removing the pins as you go.

### MACHINE PIECING PATCHES BY THE FLAG METHOD

The flag method enables you to join several pairs of patches in one go. Right sides facing, pin the patches in pairs. Stitch along the seam line using the presser foot as a guide, removing the pins as you go. Leave a short uncut thread between each pair. Remove the flags and cut into units. Join enough pairs to make up the patched piece. To avoid bulk, always press the patch seams flat to one side and not open as in dressmaking.

### JOINING PATCHES INTO ROWS

For both hand and machine piecing, make sure that the seam allowances match up perfectly before you pin and stitch the rows together. Press the seams in opposite directions to reduce bulk.

### SETTING-IN – BOX PATCHWORK

Setting-in is the term used when a patch is sewn into an angle. To make the angled piece, stitch two pieces together along the seam line, stop stitching 5mm (¼ in) from the end of the seam, and secure with back stitch. Right sides facing, pin one angled piece to the edge of the patch. Stitch from the corner out to the edge, then swing the adjacent angled piece to the other side of the patch, again stitching from the corner out. Press the two seam allowances of the set-in patch toward the angled piece.

### SASHING AND BORDERS

These are two very different things although they are cut and sewn in the same way. Sashings are fabric strips used within a design to separate individual patches, or blocks of patches. Borders go round the edges of the work to cover and hide any raw edges.

### BLOCKED BORDERS

For the long sides of a border, cut the strips the same length as the quilt. For the short sides, cut the strips the width of the quilt plus the double width of the border. Right sides facing, sew the long strips to the piece first, and then the short strips. Press the seam allowance away from the direction of quilting.

### BORDERS WITH MITRED CORNERS

Cut the border strips as above, adding an extra 5 cm (2 in) to all four for mitring, and stitch to the quilt in the usual way. To mitre a corner by hand, press a border strip down at a 45 degree angle, pin and slip stitch on the right side to secure in place. To mitre by machine, work from the wrong side, pressing all the corners back at a 45 degree angle. Pin together and stitch along the fold. Trim the seam allowance and press flat.

## LOG CABIN PATCHWORK

Always work from the middle out. Starting with a central square, pin and stitch strips to the square one by one, trimming each strip to the centre as you go. Work round the block anti-clockwise – each new strip will be slightly longer than the previous one. Continue adding strips until you reach the required size. Edge with mitred borders. Often several Log Cabin blocks are made and then stitched together to make a quilt.

# QUILTING TECHNIQUES

Quilts are made from three layers: a top piece which is decorated, a layer of wadding (batting) for warmth and a backing piece. These layers are held together with lines of stitching which can be worked in a grid, straight rows or elaborate patterns. Quilted borders, medallions, knots and detailed corners are all possible. Originally, lines of tiny running stitches were worked to offer more warmth. Modern technology and new fibres have made this unnecessary, although the stitches still need to be of equal length.

### TACKING (BASTING) QUILTS

### HAND QUILTING

### MACHINE QUILTING

Sandwich the wadding (batting) between the top piece and the backing, with the fabrics right side out. Tack (baste) together securely. Knot a long length of thread in a contrasting colour. Work from the middle out, tacking the layers together horizontally, vertically and diagonally. If quilting by machine or with a hoop, add extra lines round the edges.

Place the inner hoop on a flat surface, lay the tacked fabric on top. Place the outer hoop over both and screw the nut to tighten the hoop. Stitch from the top, using your free hand to guide the needle up and down through the layers below.

For quilting grids and straight lines, a quilting foot will allow the machine to move more easily over thick fabrics. For free-form quilting, remove the foot and lower the foot lever. Stretch the fabric taut either with a hoop or your hands, and stitch slowly so that you can accurately guide the stitches.

# Appliqué Techniques

Appliqué can be worked in a variety of fabrics, including silk, wool and cotton, and strong, closely woven fabric is possibly the best choice. Felt is popular for appliqué designs because it does not fray. Design ideas are limitless and virtually any shape can be used. Broderie perse and stained glass appliqué, together with cut and sew, inlaid and reverse appliqué methods, are just a few of the techniques featured in the book.

IRON-ON FUSIBLE BONDING WEB

### 1

A quick and easy way to attach appliqué to the fabric. The appliqué fabric is fused to the web, so it won't fray. Trace the outline on to the fusible web.

### 2

Roughly cut out the design and iron this on to the fabric. Cut around the outline with a sharp pair of scissors, a rotary cutter or craft knife.

### 3

Peel off the backing paper and iron, fusing the motif to the main fabric. Set the machine to a zig zag and stitch around the raw edge of the motif.

PIN TACKING (BASTING)

Tack (baste) the seam allowance around the appliqué design. Mark the placement lines on the right side of the fabric. Arrange the appliqué shapes on the fabric following these lines. First position the background pieces, and then layer any extra pieces on top. Alternatively, attach the pieces with double-sided tape.

*BELOW: This simple appliqué sunflower has been stitched on by hand.*

# STITCHES

· · · · · ·

Straight stitch is the standard machine sewing stitch, worked in straight lines and secured by back stitch at the end of each seam. Machine tacking stitches are worked by setting the machine to the longest stitch. To attach appliqué and crazy patchwork, set the machine to a close zig zag stitch and work a row of satin stitches. The following hand stitches are used throughout the book.

### RUNNING STITCH

This is the main stitch used for hand quilting. It is also used for sewing seams in patchwork and quilting. Stitches should be of an even length, no bigger than 3 mm (⅛ in), and can be run a few at a time. Running stitch is also used in sashiko and kantha work.

### HOLBEIN STITCH

Work a row of running stitch in one direction and then fill in the spaces on the return journey.

### SLIP-STITCH

This stitch is used to secure a finished edge to another surface, like an appliqué or a binding. With the needle, catch a thread under the fabric together with a single thread on the fold of the fabric, spacing these small stitches evenly apart.

### WHIP STITCH

Also known as oversewing and overcasting, this small straight stitch is used to hold together two edges. Work from back to front, inserting the needle at an angle and picking up a thread from each piece at the same time.

### STAB STITCH

This stitch replaces running stitch when quilting thick fabric. Hold the needle perpendicular to the fabric, and work one stitch at a time. It is also used to outline individual shapes on quilted fabric.

### BLANKET STITCH

Blanket, or buttonhole, stitch is ideal for finishing off raw or scalloped edges on fabrics that don't fray, such as felt or blanket. It can also be worked over a fold. Insert the needle into the back so that it points up to the raw edge, wind the loose thread over the needle and pull through the loop. Make a decorative feature of large blanket stitches by sewing them in a contrasting colour.

# GENERAL TECHNIQUES
· · · · · ·

FINDING THE GRAIN OF THE FABRIC

It is necessary to find the grain to straighten raw edges. Nick the fabric just below the raw edge, pull a thread gently across the fabric and cut along the line made. You can pull threads to fringe a piece of fabric and also to mark a grid. Sometimes you will need to find the straight grain in order to centre a motif.

ENLARGING A DESIGN

Trace the motif on to squared paper. On another sheet of paper, mark out the same number of squares to the required size of the finished design. Copy the motif on to the new grid so that the lines of the design correspond exactly with the original.

TRANSFERRING A DESIGN
ON TO FABRIC

<u>1</u>

Copy the design on to dressmaker's carbon paper. Place the carbon on the reverse of the fabric and then trace over the outline with a pen, pressing heavily.

<u>2</u>

Pouncing is used to transfer a design on to the right side of the fabric for an appliqué or quilting design. Trace over the design on to paper with a dressmaker's wheel or an unthreaded sewing machine, so that the design appears as a broken line. Push tailor's chalk through the pierced paper with a brush or sponge to mark the fabric.

<u>3</u>

Trace the design on to tissue paper, pin to the wrong side of the fabric then machine round the outline. Rip away the tissue paper to reveal the outline. This method is good for fine or fragile fabric.

*BELOW: This drawstring bag shows designs transferred on to the patchwork squares.*

Bias strips are used for binding, piping and also in the stained glass appliqué method. Cut a square on the straight grain, fold it in half diagonally and stitch together the open edges. Press the seam allowance flat and trim. Mark parallel lines on to the fabric and then roll it into a tube so that the top edge aligns with the first marked line. Pin and stitch along this line. Press the seam flat and trim. Cut along the marked lines into one long continuous strip of bias binding. Alternatively, cut several strips on the diagonal and then join them together, pressing the seam allowance flat.

### BINDING A MITRED CORNER

#### 1

Stitch along one edge, reducing the size of the stitches near the corner. Stop stitching 5 mm (¼ in) from the corner, lift the presser foot and swivel the quilt to stitch the next edge. A tuck will form in the binding at the corner. Lower the presser foot, and carry on stitching the next side.

#### 2

Fold over the binding, pin and sew close to the previous stitching line. Fold the tuck diagonally to mitre the corners and slip-stitch in place.

For the front, cut a square to fit the cushion pad, adding 1 cm (½ in) seam allowance on all sides. Cut a back piece 2.5 cm (1 in) bigger on one side, and then cut in half lengthways. Press, and sew a 1 cm (½ in) hem along the cut edge of both back pieces. Right sides facing, pin the front to the back pieces so that one hem lies slightly over the other. Sew round all four seams and, if directed, stitch in piping or fringing now. Clip the corners, press and turn right side out.

### STRETCHING AND MOUNTING A PICTURE

Stretch the finished piece taut over the backing. Using a strong thread, stitch back and forth, joining the raw edges in a criss cross pattern and pulling the thread tightly as you go. Work the long sides first, then repeat with the short sides. Secure to the backing board with tape.

### DRAWSTRING BAG

#### 1

Pin together two rectangles in main fabric and sew round three sides, leaving the top short side open. Cut two rectangles the same size in lining and stitch the two long sides. Stitch part way across the short end, break off for 5 cm (2 in), then stitch to the end. Right sides facing, pin the two bags together and stitch a continuous line round the top edge. Trim and clip the seam. Pull the bag through the lining. Press and slip-stitch to close the gap.

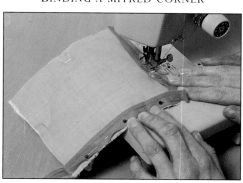

#### 2

Push the lining into the bag and press flat. For the channel, machine stitch two parallel lines, 1 cm (½ in) from the top edge and 1 cm (½ in) apart. Make a hole in the seam between the two rows of stitching with a stitch unpicker and thread the drawstring through.

# VELVET SCARF
. . . . . .

Squares arranged on the diagonal form the serrated edge to the patchwork borders on this wide scarf.
The patches are cut from both silk and velvet to create an interesting texture.

### YOU WILL NEED
. . . . . .

*thin card (cardboard)
and pencil*

*craft knife*

*dressmaker's scissors*

*scraps of silk and velvet in
pink, rust and brown*

*1 m x 90 cm
(1 yd x 36 in) velvet*

*sewing machine and
matching thread*

*iron*

*dressmaker's pins*

*1.8 m x 40 cm
(72 in x 16 in) silk lining*

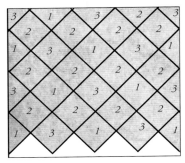

### PREPARATION

Follow the plan below. Each border uses 26 squares. Make the templates 9 cm (3½ in) square. Cut out 24 rust squares, 14 pink squares, 14 brown (velvet and silk) squares. Halve three of the pink squares and cut one diagonally into quarters. Halve six of the brown squares. Follow the plan and arrange the patches in two borders. Cut the velvet widthways and sew into a piece 2 m (2 yd) long.

KEY: 1 = BROWN
     2 = RUST
     3 = PINK

### 1

Sew the squares into strips and then join the strips into one piece (see Basic Techniques). Insert the triangles in the sides and top to make three straight edges. Press the seams. Make the second border.

### 2

Measure the borders and trim the velvet to fit. Pin the straight edge of each border to the velvet. Machine stitch close to the edge and then appliqué with a zig zag stitch. Trim and press.

### 3

Right sides facing, pin the velvet piece to the silk lining. Stitch round the seams leaving a gap on one long edge. Trim and clip the corners. Turn right side out and press. Slipstitch the opening.

# VELVET SLIPPERS

· · · · · · ·

These children's slippers are made from velvet and silk scraps. The tops have been quilted with tiny kantha stitches. These repetitive filling stitches can run in any direction and are commonly worked on Indian kantha quilts.

## YOU WILL NEED

· · · · · ·

*dressmaker's paper and pencil*

*dressmaker's scissors*

*30 cm x 90 cm*
*(12 in x 36 in) velvet*

*30 cm x 90 cm*
*(12 in x 36 in) silk*

*15 cm x 90 cm*
*(6 in x 36 in) calico*

*needle and tacking*
*(basting) thread*

*craft knife*

*pair of insoles*

*fabric marker*

*fabric glue*

*metallic thread*

*sewing machine and*
*matching thread*

*dressmaker's pins*

*pair of soles*

*4 small tassels*

## PREPARATION

Enlarge and draw the templates on to paper and cut out four slipper tops in both velvet and silk. Cut out four calico lining pieces and tack (baste) these to the reverse of the velvet. Cut a pair of insoles to size. Trace round the insoles on to a piece of velvet, adding a seam allowance and cut out.

### 1

Place the insoles on the reverse of the velvet. Clip the seam allowance and turn under. Glue the edges, pressing firmly in place.

### 2

Decorate the velvet tops with metallic thread using tiny running stitches (see Basic Techniques). Join the tops along the centre seam. Right sides facing, stitch the velvet to the silk lining along the front edge. Turn right side out and tack (baste) the raw edges.

### 3

Pin the tops to the insoles and secure with slip-stitch.

### TO FINISH

Glue the soles to the base of the slippers, hiding the turnings. Leave to dry. Sew the tassels to the slipper tops.

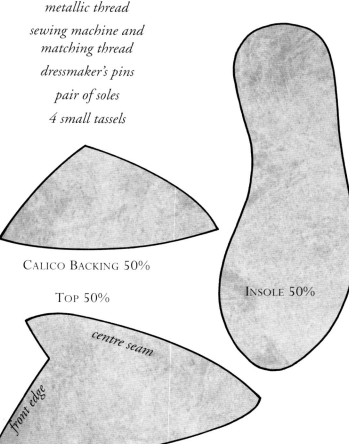

CALICO BACKING 50%

TOP 50%

*centre seam*

*front edge*

INSOLE 50%

# CRAZY PATCHWORK CUSHION
· · · · · · ·

The appliqué on this cushion looks like crazy paving. The irregularly shaped patches are arranged at random. Choose fabrics of a similar texture and with varying tonal values for a professional look.

### PREPARATION

Cut the cotton fabric into two 46 cm (18 in) squares. Enlarge the diagram and cut card (cardboard) templates to cover one square. A rough, open-textured cotton was used for the base, complemented with patches cut from scraps of furnishing fabrics with interesting, open weaves.

### TO FINISH

Press the squares flat and, right sides facing, pin the fringe to one square. Stitch into the seams as you make up the cover. Insert the zip (zipper). Insert the cushion pad.

<u>1</u>

Cut out the crazy patches from the scraps of fabric, adding a 5 mm (¼ in) turning all round.

<u>2</u>

Tack (baste) the templates to the scraps. Pin and tack to the cushion fabric.

<u>3</u>

Slip-stitch round each shape in matching thread, to secure to the base.

DIAGRAM OF WHOLE COVER 33⅓%

# HATPIN CUSHION

An appliqué of crazy patchwork, in velvet, satin and silk, has been stitched into an extra large pin cushion for storing decorative hatpins.

YOU WILL NEED

*dressmaker's scissors*

*dressmaker's paper*

*pair of compasses and pencil*

*scraps of silk, velvet and satin*

*50 cm x 90 cm*
*(20 in x 36 in) calico*

*dressmaker's pins*

*sewing machine and*
*matching threads*

*iron*

*wadding (batting)*

*needle*

## PREPARATION

Cut out the templates in paper. You will need a circular template with a diameter of 18 cm (7 in) for the base/top, and a rectangular one measuring 52 cm x 10 cm (20½ in x 4 in) for the band. Cut a silk base, and one top and one band in calico. Cut a strip on the bias in both velvet and silk measuring 52 cm x 5 cm (20½ in x 2 in).

### 1

Join the short ends of the calico band together and stitch the band to the silk base. Pin and stitch the calico top to the calico band leaving a small gap to turn through. Trim, press and fill with wadding (batting). Stitch the gap closed.

### 2

Cut out lots of random patches from the scraps. Turn under the raw edges and machine stitch the patches together, laying them over each other to make a piece of crazy patchwork. Cut out a top, using the template. Make a narrow patched strip from silk and velvet squares 52 cm (20½ in) long. Position the velvet and silk bias strips side by side and place the patched strip over the join. Pin, turn the raw edges under and machine stitch.

### 3

With right sides together, stitch the patched band to the patched top. Press and turn right side out.

### 4

Pull the outer patched cover over the inner pad, turn a hem and slip-stitch along the edge.

# CATHEDRAL WINDOW NEEDLECASE

· · · · · ·

Don't be frightened if this piece of patchwork looks complicated. It is in fact easy to construct.
This is not really a quilting method, but because the patches are layered the resulting fabric is
very warm and so the idea could be translated into a quilt.

YOU WILL NEED

· · · · · ·

*scrap of taffeta*
*dressmaker's scissors*
*iron*
*dressmaker's pins*
*needle and matching thread*
*scrap of silk organza*
*scrap of lining fabric*
*sewing machine and*
*matching thread*
*4 pieces of felt*
*pinking shears*
*button*

PREPARATION

Cut eight squares of taffeta on
the straight grain, twice the
intended size of the patch.
Press under the raw edges.

### 1

Find the centre point of each square by matching opposite corners and press on the fold.

### 2

Fold each corner to the centre point. Press and
pin in place.

### 3

Fold each corner to the centre point once more,
then press and pin. Secure the corners at the
centre with one small stitch.

### 4

Place two patches, wrong sides facing and whip
stitch across the top. Sew two rows of four
blocks in this way, and then join the rows.

### 5

Measure the fold from one corner to the centre
point of one patch. Cut ten squares to this size
in silk organza. Pin each piece diagonally over
the seam. To cover the raw edge of the organza,
roll the fold over and slip-stitch in place. Do
the same on all the folds to create the cathedral
window effect.

### 6

Cut the lining fabric to fit the case, adding a
5 mm (¼ in) seam allowance. Press under the
seam allowance. Wrong sides facing, slip-stitch
the lining to the needlecase. Sew a button on
one side and a fabric loop on the other. Cut the
felt to size and pink the edges. Stack the felt
pieces, place in the needlecase and stitch down
the centre line.

# FOLDED-STAR PIN CUSHION
• • • • • •

Although deceptively intricate, this pin cushion is easy to make. Squares are folded into triangles and then arranged on the base to make the star. Because the patches are unfitted and without seams, this technique is not classed as a true patchwork.

YOU WILL NEED
• • • • • •

*scraps of taffeta in two colours*
*dressmaker's scissors*
*iron*
*scrap of cotton fabric*
*dressmaker's pins*
*needle and matching threads*
*pair of compasses and pencil*
*scrap of velvet*
*sewing machine*
*stuffing*

## PREPARATION

Cut 12 taffeta rectangles 5 cm x 9 cm (2 in x 3½ in) in colour one, and eight the same size in colour two. Press a 5 mm (¼ in) turning along one long side of each rectangle. Cut a cotton base, 20 cm (8 in) square. Fold the opposite corners, first lengthways and then widthways into the centre of the square. Press along the fold lines.

### 1

On each rectangular patch, fold the two corners on the turned side down to the centre to form a triangle, and press.

### 3

For the second layer, arrange eight triangles in colour two round the centre point. First, pin four triangles to the base 2 cm (¾ in) from the centre, with the folded sides running parallel to the square. Then pin four diagonally so that they overlap these. Slip-stitch the outer edges.

### 2

Arrange four triangles in colour one on the centre of the base fabric, with folded sides facing, to form a square. Pin and slip-stitch the folded edges to the base.

### 4

Arrange eight triangles in colour one. Pin each triangle to the base, overlapping the previous layer, positioned 4 cm (1½ in) from the centre. Slip-stitch the triangle points to the base and tack (baste) round the outer edges.

## TO FINISH

With the compass point centred, draw a circle round the star close to the outside edge. Cut a matching circle in velvet. Right sides facing, stitch the star to the velvet. Leave a small gap to turn through. Clip and press. Turn right side out. Fill with stuffing and slip-stitch the gap.

# PATCHWORK BEAR

· · · · · ·

Soft toys, like this delightful satin bear, were often made from patchwork in days gone by. Colourful satin patches are pieced together in box patchwork and then cut into a bear shape.

YOU WILL NEED

· · · · · ·

*thin card (cardboard)
and pencil*

*craft knife*

*50 cm x 90 cm (20 in x
36 in) iron-on interfacing*

*dressmaker's scissors*

*iron*

*scraps of satin fabric in
assorted colours*

*dressmaker's pins*

*sewing machine and
matching thread*

*needle and tacking
(basting) thread*

*rotary cutter*

*stuffing*

## PREPARATION

Enlarge and make the teddy template and cut out in card (cardboard). Enlarge and make templates 1 and 2 in card and transfer to the interfacing. Cut enough for two patched pieces for the bear, cutting twice as many patches from 2. Make all of piece 1 in one fabric. Make piece 2 in assorted colours, so that there is an equal number of light and dark shades. Iron the interfacing to the fabric scraps, then cut out the patches with a 5 mm (¼ in) seam allowance. When making up each box, join one light and one dark piece so that the dark piece is always on the same side in order to create the illusion of depth.

### 1

Right sides facing, join one light and one dark piece 2 to form an angle. Press the seam to one side. Pin piece 1 to the angled patch matching the corners. Stitch from one corner in the middle of the angle to the end of the seam and cut the threads. Swivel the adjacent angled piece to the other edge of piece 1 and pin. Stitch from the centre point to the end of the seam (for setting-in see Basic Techniques).

### 2

Make lots of boxes and stitch them together in horizontal rows. Press the seams in one direction only. Carefully tack (baste) the horizontal rows of box patchwork together and stitch. Press the seams in opposite directions (see Basic Techniques).

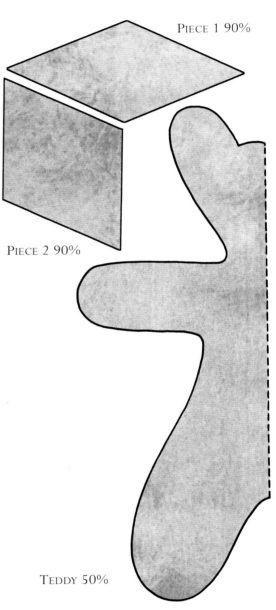

PIECE 1 90%

PIECE 2 90%

TEDDY 50%

### TO FINISH

Make two patched pieces large enough for the bear. Cut out two bears without a seam allowance in interfacing. Iron to the wrong side of each patch. Fold the patch in half and pin the template along the fold line, adding a seam allowance. Cut out two pieces the same in box patchwork with a rotary cutter. Right sides facing, starting on an inside leg, stitch round the shape leaving 5 cm (2 in) open. Clip into the corners, trim and press. Turn right side out, fill with stuffing and slip-stitch the gap.

# VELVET THROW

This project shows how to make a patched piece of velvet. Pairs of triangles are sewn into diamonds and then grouped into stars. The patchwork could easily be made into a quilt or a cushion.

## PREPARATION

Measure the size required for the patch. Draw a triangle, with a base half the length of the other sides, and transfer on to card (cardboard). Work out how many templates will be needed and cut out in interfacing using a craft knife. Iron to the wrong side of the velvet and cut out the pieces with a 5 mm (¼ in) seam allowance. Arrange the cut triangles and manipulate into diamonds with the best design possibility. Combine the diamonds to make stars, using colour carefully. Draw a plan for reference.

### 1

Pin and stitch pairs of triangles together along the short edge to form a diamond, using the flag method (see Basic Techniques). Cut joining threads and press the seams flat.

### 2

Stitch the pairs together in horizontal strips following your own colour scheme, and then join the strips together to make up the finished piece. Press the seams in opposite directions to reduce bulk (see Basic Techniques).

## TO FINISH

To make the patched piece into a throw, cut a piece of silk lining to fit. Right sides facing, stitch round the seam line, leaving a 10 cm (4 in) gap. Clip the corners and press. Turn right side out and slip-stitch the opening. To make a quilt or cushion cover, see Basic Techniques for instructions.

# SUITING THROW

· · · · · ·

This gentleman's throw is made out of scraps of suiting fabrics bought from a tailor. The scraps are cut into rectangles so that the stripes and patterns run in as many directions as possible.

### YOU WILL NEED

· · · · · ·

*thin card (cardboard)
and pencil*

*craft knife*

*scraps of suiting*

*dressmaker's pencil*

*dressmaker's scissors*

*dressmaker's pins*

*sewing machine and
matching thread*

*silk lining in a
contrasting colour*

*needle and matching thread*

*iron*

*tacking (basting) thread*

*shirt buttons*

### PREPARATION

Cut a rectangular template in card (cardboard) and calculate the number of patches required. Transfer the template to the suiting using a dressmaker's pencil. Cut out the patches with a 5 mm (¼ in) seam allowance. Pin and stitch together in pairs using the flag method (see Basic Techniques). Stitch the pairs in horizontal rows and press the seams.

### 1

Join the horizontal strips of suiting together to make a large patched piece. Trim the seams and press in opposite directions to reduce bulk (see Basic Techniques).

### 2

Measure the patch and add 13 cm (5 in) all round for a loose border. Cut the silk lining to this measurement. Right sides facing, pin the lining to the patched piece and stitch 1 cm (½ in) from the edge. Leave a 10 cm (4 in) opening on one side and the corners free. Press the seam and pull through. Slip-stitch the gap.

### 3

Iron a loose and even fold of silk around the border. Pin and tack (baste) in place.

### TO FINISH

Top stitch in matching thread close to the seam line between the suiting and the silk. Mitre the corners and slip-stitch (see Basic Techniques). Sew the shirt buttons round the border, as shown.

# LAVENDER BAG

· · · · · ·

Stars are frequently found in patchwork and the LeMoyne Star is a popular choice. To achieve this tricky eight-seam join that meets in the centre of the star, work slowly and carefully.

## YOU WILL NEED

· · · · · ·

*tracing paper and pencil*

*thin (card) cardboard*

*craft knife*

*scraps of silk organza in three colours*

*rotary cutter*

*scrap of lining silk*

*dressmaker's pins*

*sewing machine and matching thread*

*needle and matching thread*

*dried lavender*

*ribbon*

## PREPARATION

Trace the star and make the templates. For each star (you will need two), cut out eight pieces from template 1 in two colours and four pieces each from templates 2 and 3 in the third colour. Use a rotary cutter, if wished.

### 1

To make the star, with right sides facing, pin together two of piece 1, in two colours, and stitch. Make another pair to match. Press flat.

### 2

Join the two pairs together, carefully matching the centre seams, pin and stitch. Press the seam flat to one side. Make the other half of the star in the same way.

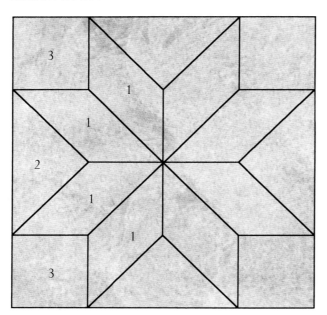

### 3

To set in the square 3, swivel the square to match the corner points and pin to the angled edge (see Basic Techniques). To set in the triangle 2, match the corner points and pin to the angled edge. Stitch and press.

## TO FINISH

Set in three more squares, and three more triangles to make the patch. Make a second patch the same. Measure one side and cut two pieces of organza this length plus 5 cm (2 in) wide. Stitch one to the top of each patch and press. Right sides facing, stitch round the base and sides of the bag and turn through. Fold a 1 cm (½ in) hem round the top of the bag, press and top stitch. Fill the bag with dried lavender and tie with a ribbon bow.

## LeMoyne Star

# NIGHTDRESS CASE

This patchwork design is traditionally used on quilts to celebrate a marriage. The curved lines meet and overlap at regular intervals, giving the overall impression of two interlocking rings.

YOU WILL NEED

*thin card (cardboard)*

*craft knife*

*dressmaker's scissors*

*scraps of organza in
five colours*

*dressmaker's pins*

*sewing machine and
matching thread*

*iron*

*needle and matching thread*

*press studs (snap fasteners)*

PREPARATION

Make the templates from the back of the book. Each wedding ring design is made up of eight arcs, four patches 4 and one centre 5, and you will need six wedding rings in total. For each arc, cut four of section 1 in the first colour. Cut 32 of 1. For each arc, cut two of section 2 in the second colour. Cut 16 of 2. For four arcs only, cut one of section 3 in colour four, and cut one of section 3 in colour five. Cut eight of 3. Cut two of 4 in the second, and two of 4 in the third colour. Cut two of 5 in the fourth, and two of 5 in the fifth colour.

### 1

To make an arc, pin together and stitch four pieces of section 1. Press seams to one side. Pin and stitch one piece of section 2 at each end of the arc.

### 3

For the four remaining arcs, pin and stitch section 3 at each end of the arc, in two contrasting colours. Press seams to one side.

### 5

Take section 5 and match the notch to the centre seam on one of the oval patches, align the corners and stitch. Press the seam towards the oval. Pin the second oval piece to the other curved edge of 5, matching the centre points and alternating the colours of the patches. Stitch and press towards the oval.

### 2

Take section 4 and match the notch to the centre seam of one arc, and align the end pieces to the points of 2. Pin and stitch. Make three more patches the same.

### 4

Match the centre seam of one patched arc to the notch on 4. Pin and stitch. Press the seam to the arc. Make four patches in the same way.

TO FINISH

Join a second piece 5 to the curved edge of the second oval as before and continue to make a square. Measure the square, add a 1 cm (½ in) seam allowance on three sides and a 2 cm (¾ in) seam allowance on the other. Cut a piece of organza to fit. Halve the long edge and cut. Press under a double hem on both pieces and stitch. Overlap the two pieces, right sides to the patched piece and make an envelope cover (see Basic Techniques). Make a silk lining in the same way, if wished. Stitch pairs of press studs (snap fasteners) to the opening.

# CORDED PURSE

Corded quilting is a very old technique that was popular in Italy and so became known as Italian quilting. The fabric is quilted in parallel lines to make channels, which are then threaded with cord or yarn to form raised lines. This method is often used with trapunto quilting.

### YOU WILL NEED
. . . . . .

*tissue paper and marker pen*

*30 cm x 90 cm
(12 in x 36 in) muslin*

*fabric marker*

*needle and tacking
(basting) thread*

*30 cm x 90 cm
(12 in x 36 in) bronze satin*

*sewing machine and
matching thread*

*cord or yarn*

*flat blunt needle*

*dressmaker's pins*

*30 cm x 90 cm
(12 in x 36 in) blue satin*

*dressmaker's scissors*

*press stud (snap fastener)*

### PREPARATION

Trace the design on to tissue paper. Tack (baste) the muslin to the wrong side of the bronze satin and stitch round the edge. Pin the template to the muslin and stitch the design. Cut and secure the ends and remove the template.

CORDED DESIGN 25%

### 1

Use the flat blunt needle to thread the cord or yarn through the channels. Pull the yarn out at the corners and leave a loop so as not to tighten and distort the fabric.

### 2

Right sides facing, pin to the blue satin. Stitch round the flap and across the opposite end. Clip and press to the right side. Slip-stitch the sides. Sew on the press stud (snap fastener).

# CORDED QUILT

· · · · · ·

This method of quilting is worked by stitching the outline of a design in two parallel lines on to two layers of cloth. This creates channels which are then filled. This method can be worked all over for a whole cloth, or it can simply be used to make decorative borders.

YOU WILL NEED
· · · · · ·

*dressmaker's scissors*

*satin fabric*

*muslin*

*tissue paper and pencil*

*dressmaker's pins*

*needle and tacking (basting) thread*

*sewing machine and matching thread*

*flat blunt needle*

*woollen yarn*

*calico for lining*

### PREPARATION

Decide on the size of your quilt and cut the satin and muslin to fit. Trace the design on to tissue paper several times until you have enough to make a complete border. Tack (baste) the muslin to the wrong side of the satin fabric and stitch round the quilt, close to the edge.

### 1

Pin the template to the muslin. Stitch the design in even parallel lines either side of the outline. Cut and secure the ends and remove the template.

### 2

Thread the flat needle with yarn and insert it into a channel working the yarn between both layers of fabric. To turn a corner, bring out the needle to the wrong side, make a loop and then push back into the channel. Where two channels cross, cut the yarn and then continue on the other side. Fill the border of the quilt in this way.

### TO FINISH

Trim the satin and muslin and cut the lining to fit. Right sides facing, stitch together, leaving a 10 cm (4 in) opening. Turn right sides out and slip-stitch the opening.

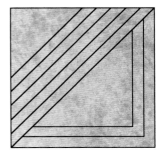

ONE-QUARTER OF DESIGN SHOWN. ENLARGE TO SIZE REQUIRED FOR QUILT.

# SHADOW PICTURE

· · · · · ·

Shadow quilting is another form of trapunto work. This delightful child's picture is made from coloured shapes applied to a base. These are then covered with a transparent fabric, producing a delicate, shadowy effect.

25%

## YOU WILL NEED

· · · · · ·

*paper and marker pen*

*dressmaker's scissors*

*double-sided tape*

*white, light and dark orange, and light and dark green felt squares*

*2 pieces muslin, each 38 cm x 30 cm (15 in x 12 in)*

*dressmaker's pins*

*needle and tacking (basting) thread*

*embroidery frame*

*white, orange, green and brown embroidery thread*

*crewel embroidery needle*

*iron*

*backing board*

*sticky tape*

*picture frame*

### PREPARATION

Enlarge the design on to paper, drawing the flower centres and the ladybird separately. Cut out all the pieces and stick them to the felt with double-sided tape. Draw round the shapes and cut out.

### 1

Lay a piece of muslin over the original drawing. Peel off the backing paper and position the felt pieces on the muslin. Place the second piece of muslin on top. Pin and tack (baste) the layers together.

### 2

Fit the work into an embroidery frame. Using a single strand of thread, stitch round all of the shapes in Holbein stitch (see Basic Techniques). Work details on to the snail, ladybird and flower centre in contrasting colours.

### TO FINISH

Remove the quilting from the embroidery frame and press carefully on the reverse side. Use a backing board in a complementary colour to enhance the shadow quilting. Stretch the piece over the backing board, and tape it to the back. Place in a frame.

# CAMEO PICTURE
· · · · · · ·

This popular appliqué idea is fun to make. Copy a silhouette from a book or a piece of china and for unashamed plagiarism use a Wedgwood blue backing. A photograph of someone you know can also be used, so long as it is in profile. Mount the finished cameo in a frame or, alternatively, make a brooch following the instructions for the Gothic Jewels project.

### YOU WILL NEED
· · · · · ·

*marker pen*

*fine white or black iron-on interfacing*

*dressmaker's scissors*

*iron*

*blue backing material*

*embroidery hoop*

*sewing machine and matching thread*

*small frame*

<u>1</u>

Trace the silhouette on to the interfacing. Cut out and iron on to the backing fabric.

<u>2</u>

Stretch the backing material on an embroidery hoop. Remove the presser foot from your sewing machine and stitch round the outline. Add decorative details to the collar and hair to complete the design.

### TO FINISH

Mount the finished cameo picture in a small frame (see Basic Techniques).

# MIRROR FRAME
· · · · · ·

A patched fabric frame has been made from pieces of bronze silk, satin and organza. A quilted design
and hand embroidery add a decorative touch.

## PREPARATION

Enlarge the templates from
the back of the book and cut
out in paper. Cut three strips
from each of the bronze
fabrics 40 cm (16 in) long.
Vary the widths of the strips
slightly, but plan so that when
stitched together the combined width of all the strips is
50 cm (20 in). Cut out a
backing board 3, in thick card
(cardboard). Trace round the
edge of 3, and from this cut a
10 cm (4 in) wide facing in
bronze silk. Cut a piece 2
from the remaining silk.

### 1

Stitch together the satin, silk and organza
strips, alternating the fabrics, and press the
seams flat. From this, cut out piece 1 twice for
the sides of the frame.

### 3

Right sides facing, pin the centre piece to the
end sections and stitch. Clip the curves and
trim the organza.

### 2

Cut out piece 2 in silk and place right sides
facing the organza for the centre piece. Pin and
stitch round the inner circle. Clip and trim.
Turn right side out and press.

### 4

Tack (baste) the fabric to the wadding (batting)
and trim to size. Enlarge and trace the quilted
pattern from piece 3 on to tissue paper. Pin the
paper to the fabric and machine stitch the
design using matching thread. Add the stars
freehand using gold thread. Pin and stitch the
silk facing to the whole piece. Clip and press.

### TO FINISH

Centre the mirror on the backing board 3 and
glue. Cover the backing with the fabric frame.
Fold the facing over to the wrong side of the
backing and glue in place.

# MEDIEVAL QUILT

This medieval-inspired quilt makes use of a harmonious colour scheme of frosty blues, soft golds and antique creams in glazed cotton, satin, brocade and moiré. The patches can be quilted individually, which is especially useful on a large-scale project such as this.

## YOU WILL NEED
• • • • • •

*paper and pencil*

*dressmaker's scissors*

*fabric scraps in glazed cotton, brocade, satin and moiré*

*iron*

*dressmaker's pins*

*sewing machine and matching thread*

*calico*

*wadding (batting)*

*needle and tacking (basting) thread*

*thin card (cardboard)*

*craft knife*

*iron-on fusible bonding web*

*fabric scraps in metallic tissue and iridescent organza*

*crewel needle and thick metallic thread*

*beads and sequins*

PLAN AND TEMPLATES 25%

## TO FINISH

To join the panels together, turn under the raw edges on the front and back and pin together. Zig zag the panels together from the back. Cut strips of calico about 5 cm (2 in) wide and as wide and as long as the quilt. Press under a turning along the long edges. Position the strips over the panel joins and top stitch to the front of the quilt using zig zag stitch. Make a border using calico and top stitch to the quilt in the same way.

## PREPARATION

This quilt is made up of 36 cm (14 in) square panels. Half of the panels have a large central diamond design and the other half are divided into four with either four diamond designs or two diamond and two square. Make a plan of the quilt and plan the colour fall. Enlarge the diagram and cut out a diamond template in both sizes, a triangular template in both sizes and a square template from paper. Cut out as many fabric patches as you need, adding a turning all round. Press under the turnings. Pin the patches together to form panels and machine together using zig zag stitch. Cut out the same number of panels in calico and wadding (batting). Sandwich the wadding between the patched fabric and the calico and tack (baste). Machine quilt the panels using zig zag stitch.

### 1
Enlarge and transfer the animal motifs from the back of the book to thin card (cardboard) and cut out. Iron the bonding web to the wrong side of the iridescent and metallic scraps. Cut out an animal motif for each panel with a large diamond design.

### 2
Peel off the backing paper and iron the motifs to the panels, then embellish with metallic thread, beads and sequins.

### 3
Hand quilt details on some of the panels using the thick metallic thread. On other panels, wrong side facing, machine quilt using thick metallic thread in the bobbin and regular thread on top.

# QUILTED WAISTCOAT

· · · · · ·

The paisley motif originated in India and was brought to Europe by the East India Company
in the 18th century. A paisley design has been painted on to the waistcoat fronts
and then each shape is hand quilted in stab stitch.

## YOU WILL NEED
· · · · · ·

*commercial waistcoat pattern*

*dressmaker's scissors*

*calico*

*black lining fabric*

*vanishing marker*

*gold gutta outliner*

*black, green and purple
silk paint*

*paintbrush*

*wadding (batting)*

*needle and tacking
(basting) thread*

*sewing machine and
matching thread*

## PREPARATION

Cut out the waistcoat back
and fronts in both calico and
lining material. Enlarge the
template from the back of the
book and transfer the paisley
design on to the calico fronts
with the vanishing marker.

### 1

Outline the paisley design
with the gold gutta outliner.
Leave to dry overnight.

### 2

Fill in the pattern using the
silk paints. Work one colour
at a time and leave it to dry
before starting the next
colour. Then fill in the background colour.

### 3

Sandwich the wadding (batting) between the calico and
the lining and tack (baste) in
place. Work stab stitch round
each motif to make it stand
out (see Basic Techniques).

## TO FINISH

Make up the waistcoat following the instructions with the
commercial pattern.

# QUILTED POCKET

A small project like this pocket is a good way to start quilting. Sew the finished pocket on to a plain shirt or a pyjama jacket.

## YOU WILL NEED
• • • • • •

*two 10 cm ( 4 in) squares peach fabric*

*two 10 cm (4 in) squares blue fabric*

*sewing machine and matching thread*

*iron-on interfacing*

*marker pen*

*dressmaker's pins*

*wadding (batting)*

*needle and tacking (basting) thread*

*dressmaker's scissors*

*fabric scraps*

*sequins and beads*

*calico*

## PREPARATION

Enlarge the pocket template. Machine stitch the squares of fabric into a patched piece, alternating the colours.

POCKET AND MOTIF 25%

### 1

Enlarge and trace the motif on to the interfacing. Pin the interfacing to the wadding (batting), then machine stitch round the outline of the pocket. Tack (baste) the prepared wadding to the patch.

### 2

Machine stitch parallel lines round the inner sides of each fabric square. Machine stitch around the outline of the pocket and trim.

### 3

On the interfacing side, tack round the outline of the motif. Cut out the pieces for the motif in fabric scraps and hand appliqué to the pocket. Decorate with hand stitches and an assortment of sequins and beads.

## TO FINISH

Cut the calico to fit the pocket and, right sides facing, stitch the calico back to the patched pocket leaving a small gap. Trim and clip the corners, turn right side out and press. Slip-stitch the opening. Position on the garment, and top stitch. Alternatively, if you are making the whole garment, the pocket back can be cut and applied as it is constructed.

# TRAPUNTO BOX
. . . . . .

Trapunto, a very old art form, is by far the most admired form of quilting. Outlines are stitched to the fabric and then filled from the back. Quilt a Tudor rose in this way to cover a box lid.

### YOU WILL NEED
. . . . . .

*dressmaker's scissors*

*40 m x 90 cm*
*(16 in x 36 in) blue satin*

*30 cm x 90 cm*
*(12 in x 36 in) calico*

*18 cm (7 in) hexagonal box*

*dressmaker's pins*

*needle and tacking*
*(basting) thread*

*vanishing marker*

*sticky back felt*

*sewing machine and*
*gold thread*

*wadding (batting)*

*fabric glue*

*50 cm (20 in) braid*

### PREPARATION

Cut the satin 40 cm (16 in) square. Cut a piece of calico the same size as the lid, and centre on the reverse side of the satin. Tack (baste) to secure in place. Enlarge and trace the template and draw the centred outline on to the satin with the vanishing marker. Draw round the base and sides of the box and round the base of the lid on to the sticky back felt. Cut out.

### 1
Machine stitch the outline of the Tudor rose in gold thread.

### 2
Slash the calico back of one petal and fill with wadding (batting). Stitch up the slit. Repeat on all shapes until the rose is full.

### 3
Centre the quilted design on the lid and glue. Stretch the satin over the lid and sides and stick the edges to the inside of the lid. Trim any excess. Cover the box in satin. Line the box with the sticky back felt. Glue the braid round the base of the box and round the lid.

50%

# QUILTED BOX

The method used for the box lid illustrates simple machine quilting. Wadding (batting) is sandwiched between two layers and held together by the stitched outline of the diamond and fleur-de-lys motif.

## YOU WILL NEED
••••••

*vanishing marker*

*50 m x 90 cm*
*(20 in x 36 in) gold satin*

*small rectangular box*

*wadding (batting)*

*dressmaker's scissors*

*needle and tacking*
*(basting) thread*

*sticky back felt*

*sewing machine and*
*matching thread*

*fabric glue*

50%

## PREPARATION

Enlarge the template and transfer the design with the vanishing marker on to a piece of gold satin, cut slightly larger than the lid. Cut the wadding (batting) to fit the lid. Centre and tack (baste) to the satin. Draw round the base of the box and lid on to the sticky back felt. Cut out.

### 1
Machine stitch the outline of the design.

### 2
Glue the wadding (batting) to the lid. Fold the satin over the edge and inside the lid. Mitre the corners and glue. Cover the box in satin.

### 3
Attach the sticky back felt to the lid and the base of the box.

# QUILTED HAT
. . . . . .

This pull-on hat is made from wool and silk. The raised trapunto quilting on the hat band, in the form of diamonds, is embellished with bronze thread.

YOU WILL NEED
. . . . . .

*thin card (cardboard)
and pencil*

*craft knife*

*dressmaker's paper*

*dressmaker's scissors*

*50 cm x 90 cm
(20 in x 36 in) calico*

*50 cm x 90 cm
(20 in x 36 in) pink wool*

*50 cm x 90 cm
(20 in x 36 in) pink silk*

*sewing machine and
matching thread*

*iron*

*dressmaker's pins*

*wadding (batting)*

*crewel needle and bronze
thread*

*1 m x 90 cm
(1 yd x 36 in) silk lining*

*needle and tacking
(basting) thread*

*50 cm x 2.5 cm
(20 in x 1 in) petersham*

### PREPARATION

Enlarge and cut out the motif templates in card (cardboard). Enlarge the hat templates from the back of the book and cut out piece 1 in calico and wool. Cut piece 2 in calico and silk. Cut crown piece 3 in wool and calico. Stitch pieces 1 and 2 together to make the hat band, first in calico, and then in wool and silk, taking a 1.5 cm (½ in) seam allowance. Clip and press the seams.

### 1
Draw round the templates on to the calico hat band, alternating the motif templates and spacing them evenly.

### 2
Stitch the ends of the hat band together and press. Wrong sides facing, pin the bands together and stitch round the motifs through both layers of fabric.

### 3
Wrong sides facing, pin together the two crown pieces. Pin and stitch to the quilted hat band. Turn right side out and top stitch close to the crown seam.

### 4
Turn inside out and carefully slash the calico behind each motif. Fill each motif with wadding (batting) then stitch closed. Embroider the diamonds with bronze stars. Make up a lining using the same pattern pieces and slip stitch in position.

### 5
Tack (baste) the petersham band to the lower inside edge of the hat. Stitch and press under.

DIAMOND MOTIFS
50%

# STRING PATCHWORK FRAME

String patchwork is created by sewing similiar lengths of fabric of different widths into one piece.
Interesting effects are made by adjusting the angle of the strips and by making chevron shapes.

YOU WILL NEED
• • • • • •

*black and white satin*

*dressmaker's scissors*

*sewing machine and
matching thread*

*two squares of thin card
(cardboard)*

*craft knife*

*double-sided tape*

*masking tape*

*self-adhesive felt*

*needle*

<u>1</u>

Cut the satin into narrow strips, varying the widths slightly. Right sides facing, machine stitch the strips together. Adjust the angles of the strips to make interesting effects.

<u>2</u>

Cut a window from one square of card (cardboard). Cut the patch into four sections to fit each side of the frame, allowing for a turning. Mitre the corners (see Basic Techniques).

TO FINISH

Stick the fabric to the frame with double-sided tape. Fold the raw ends to the inside and secure with masking tape. Cover the backing square with self-adhesive felt cut to size. Slip-stitch the front and back of the frame together round three sides.

# STAINED GLASS APPLIQUÉ CUSHION

This cushion has been worked using the overlay method of appliqué. Keep design ideas bold and simple. It is also important that each shape within the design is not too small.

### YOU WILL NEED
• • • • •

*thin card (cardboard) and marker pen*

*48 cm (19 in) square red silk*

*dressmaker's pins*

*dressmaker's scissors*

*scraps of yellow and green silk*

*iron*

*iron-on interfacing*

*sewing machine and matching threads*

*tracing paper*

*transfer pencil*

*two 48 cm (19 in) squares black silk*

*craft knife*

*45 cm (18 in) square cushion pad*

*needle and matching thread*

### PREPARATION

Enlarge and transfer the template to the card (cardboard). Place the template over the red silk square and transfer the star outline, following the dotted lines, using pin prick marks. Cut along the pin pricks, without cutting the outer red frame. Make a template for each diamond shape and the centre piece, following the dotted lines. Draw round the templates on to the silk scraps. Cut four yellow and four green diamonds, and one red centre piece. Iron one piece of interfacing to the red frame.

### 1

Arrange the yellow and green diamonds and the red centre piece on the interfacing. Pin and iron in place. Machine stitch in place.

### 2

Following the continuous lines, trace the black frame on to tracing paper with a transfer pencil. Turn over and iron on to the second piece of interfacing. Iron the interfacing to the wrong side of one of the black silk squares. Cut out each diamond with a craft knife, leaving a small turning on all sides. Pin and press the turnings.

### 3

Pin the black frame on top of the appliqué star and machine along all the edges.

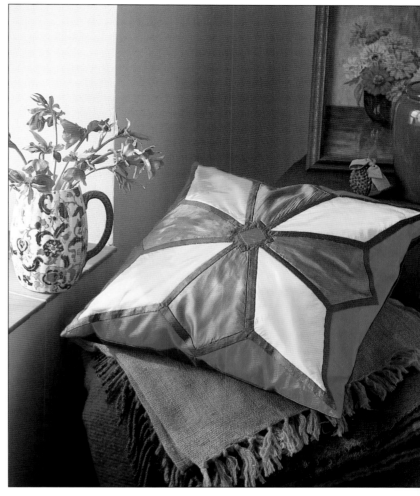

### TO FINISH

Right sides facing, place the appliqué patch to the second black silk square and stitch a seam 1 cm (½ in) from the edges. Leave an opening. Clip the corners, press and turn right side out. Insert the cushion pad and slip-stitch the opening.

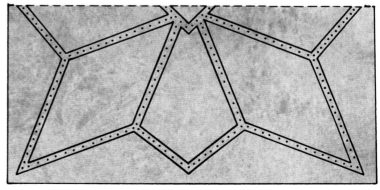

HALF OF PLAN SHOWN 25%

# SILKEN BAG
. . . . . .

This delicate piece of quilted silk sports a design of hearts, vine leaves and a bow surrounded by small running stitches. The finished quilt is sewn into a tiny drawstring bag.

YOU WILL NEED
. . . . . .

*dressmaker's scissors*

*40 cm x 90 cm
(16 in x 36 in) lining silk*

*40 cm x 90 cm
(16 in x 36 in) calico*

*tracing paper and pencil*

*8 cm x 30 cm (3 in x 12 in)
wadding (batting)*

*needle and tacking
(basting) thread*

*crewel needle and white
perlé thread*

*sewing machine and
matching thread*

*50 cm (20 in) cream
silk ribbon*

### PREPARATION

Cut two pieces of lining silk and calico measuring 23 cm x 30 cm (9 in x 12 in). Enlarge and trace the design and transfer to one piece of silk. Sandwich the wadding (batting) between the two pieces of calico, positioning the wadding where you want the quilted design. Place the marked silk on top and tack (baste) the layers together.

### 1
Outline the heart, vine and bow design in stab stitch (see Basic Techniques).

### 2
Work tiny running stitches round the design until the whole area has been covered.

REPEAT VINE AND HEART MOTIF ON
OTHER SIDE OF BOW  50 %

### TO FINISH

Cut 10 cm (4 in) diameter circle from lining silk and calico for the base of the bag. Make a lined drawstring bag using the remaining piece of lining silk and the base pieces (see Basic Techniques). For the channel, stitch two parallel lines 1 cm (½ in) apart with the top one 1 cm (½ in) from the edge. Thread and knot the silk ribbon.

# BRODERIE PERSE APPLIQUÉ NAPKINS

This once popular craft was thought to closely resemble Persian embroidery. As it developed, more and more images were incorporated into the designs. A rose has been combined with a gardening fork to create these charming napkins.

## YOU WILL NEED

*tracing paper and pencil*

*scraps of plain grey, and pink and green floral chintz fabric*

*dressmaker's scissors*

*4 linen napkins*

*dressmaker's pins*

*needle and tacking (basting) thread*

*sewing machine and matching thread*

*iron*

## PREPARATION

Transfer the fork template from the back of the book to the grey fabric. Add a small seam allowance and cut out. Cut out a flower shape, such as a rose, with a stem from chintz fabric, adding a small seam allowance.

### 1

Position the flower on a napkin with the stem entwined in the prongs of the fork. Pin and tack (baste) through the middle of the motifs. Turn under and tack a small turning and clip the edges as you work round the motifs.

### 2

Hand or machine stitch round the edges of the motifs to secure.

## TO FINISH

Embellish all four napkins in the same way. Remove the tacking (basting) threads and press carefully. Embroider thorns on the rose stem in tiny stitches if desired.

# BRODERIE PERSE
# APPLIQUÉ TABLECLOTH
· · · · · ·

The technique of cutting out a design in printed cloth to appliqué to a fabric base grew out of both necessity and the desire to preserve old favourites. Appliqué chintz fabric with a large, floral motif to a linen cloth for an antique appearance.

## YOU WILL NEED
· · · · · ·

*dressmaker's scissors*

*Irish linen*

*dressmaker's pins*

*needle and tacking (basting) thread*

*sewing machine and matching thread*

*scraps of pink and green floral chintz fabric*

*iron*

*needle and matching thread*

## PREPARATION

Cut the linen to the shape and size you require. Turn under a small hem and stitch.

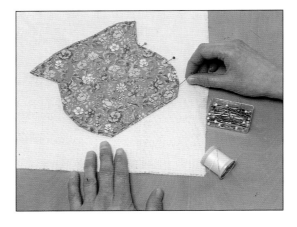

### 1

Draw a vase shape on to a scrap of chintz and cut out. Press under a small hem. Pin and tack (baste) to the corner of the cloth.

### 2

Cut a border in contrasting chintz. Press under a hem, pin and tack to the vase.

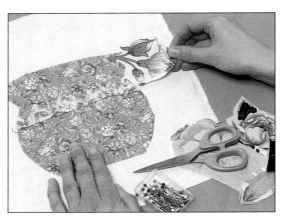

### 3

Cut out several flower shapes and leaves. Arrange in the vase, pin and tack in place.

### 4

Clip and turn the edges as you sew the motif to the cloth. When the shapes overlap each other, be sure to sew the base one first.

# SILK DRESS

· · · · · ·

This technique uses up scraps of patterned silk. The silk patches are randomly joined into panels with French seams. The idea is to make enough patched squares to sew into a large piece of fabric, which is then made into a dress. Dye the dress a strong colour to unify the design.

You Will Need
· · · · · ·

*dressmaker's paper and pencil*

*dressmaker's scissors*

*scraps of fine silk or silk scarves*

*dressmaker's pins*

*sewing machine and matching thread*

*iron*

*commercial dress pattern*

*cold water dye*

### Preparation

The panels measure 26 cm (10 in) square and they can be made up of patches following either or both diagrams. Enlarge the two diagrams and make templates for each shape and size of patch. Cut out patches from scraps of silk, allowing for a 1 cm (½ in) seam allowance on sides.

### Dress Panels

13 cm (5 in)     13 cm (5 in)

26 cm (10 in)

8 cm (3 in)   10 cm (4 in)   8 cm (3 in)

26 cm (10 in)

### 1

Using the flag method (see Basic Techniques), pin the patches in pairs with wrong sides facing. Machine and press the seams to one side. To make French seams, trim one edge back close to the stitching line. Press a small turning on the uncut edges, fold over again to cover the stitch line and press. Pin and stitch along the new fold.

### 2

Join the patches into panels, and the panels together in the same way to make a large piece of patched fabric.

### To Finish

Cut out and make the dress following the instructions with the commercial dress pattern. Make up the cold dye solution, following the manufacturer's instructions. Then scrunch the dress up and dye.

# CHILD'S SKIRT

Patches and strips of contrasting silk fabrics are sewn together in a creative mix to make this skirt. The appliqué silk patches sewn round the hemline add to the historic feel.

## YOU WILL NEED
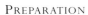

*thin perspex and marker*

*craft knife*

*dressmaker's scissors*

*1.2 m x 115 cm (47 in x 45 in) floral silk*

*scraps of contrasting silks*

*iron*

*dressmaker's pins*

*sewing machine and matching thread*

*needle and tacking (basting) thread*

*six buttons*

## PREPARATION

Enlarge and make the templates in perspex. Cut the floral fabric in half lengthwise. Cut two strips of contrasting silk 7 cm x 1.2 m (2½ in x 47 in), and press a 1 cm (½ in) seam allowance along the long edge. Cut four side strips in the same fabric, each 5 cm x 55 cm (2 in x 22 in).

## TO FINISH

Halve the waist measurement and make two waistbands. Check the length of the skirt and trim if necessary. Gather the skirt on to the waistbands and top stitch. Make buttonholes and sew on the buttons.

### 1

Pin the templates to the silk scraps and cut out. Press under the seam allowances on patches.

### 2

Machine stitch one long strip to the wrong side of one piece of floral silk. Press over to the right side and top stitch. Repeat for the second piece. Attach the side strips in the same way.

### 3

Arrange the patches on the lower edge of the skirt, pin and tack (baste) in place. Machine stitch close to the edge.

50%

# SATIN HANDBAG
· · · · · ·

This classic handbag is made from a piece of quilted satin. It has self-made handles and a quilted base for extra strength. Chose an unusual brass button to fasten the bag.

### YOU WILL NEED
· · · · · ·

*40 cm x 60 cm (16 in x 24 in) heavy interfacing*

*vanishing marker*

*dressmaker's scissors*

*40 cm x 60 cm (16 in x 24 in) wadding (batting)*

*40 cm x 60 cm (16 in x 24 in) satin*

*46 cm x 30 cm (18 in x 12 in) lining fabric*

*dressmaker's pins*

*sewing machine and matching thread*

*needle and tacking (basting) thread*

*iron*

*brass button*

### PREPARATION

Transfer the bag design from the back of the book to the interfacing. Cut out a piece of wadding (batting) to fit, and cut out the satin and a lining piece, adding a seam allowance on all sides. Sandwich the wadding between the marked interfacing and the satin, then pin and stitch round the edge. Machine quilt the grid. Cut out two satin and two lining side pieces and two satin handles, all with a seam allowance. Cut out an interfacing base 16 cm x 7 cm (6½ in x 2¾ in).

<u>1</u>

Position and tack (baste) the interfacing base to the bag. Trim the raw edges.

<u>2</u>

Make a narrow silk rouleau 5 cm x 20 cm (2 in x 8 in). Pin to the right side of the flap, with the loop pointing outwards. Make it big enough to fit the button. Right sides facing, pin the lining to the bag and stitch just inside the machine line, leaving an opening to turn through. Turn and slip-stitch closed.

<u>3</u>

Right sides facing, place satin and lining side pieces together in pairs. Machine round three sides, then turn through one long edge. Fold in half lengthwise and press. Machine stitch along fold to within 4 cm (1½ in) of the lower edge.

<u>4</u>

Top stitch round the base, the flap fold and the front edge of the bag.

<u>5</u>

Fold the handles in half lengthwise and press under a 1 cm (½ in) turning on both long sides and top stitch to 2.5 cm (1 in) of both ends. Open out the ends and top stitch to the bag.

### TO FINISH

Slip-stitch the side pieces into the bag. Sew on a decorative button.

# GOTHIC JEWELS

A plain velvet hat becomes a beautiful item of head wear when trimmed with sparkling Gothic jewels, made from machine embroidery and beads. The jewels do take time to make, however the extra effort is well worth the final result.

## YOU WILL NEED
......

*marker pen*
*scraps of water soluble fabric*
*embroidery hoop*
*thick and fine metallic thread*
*sewing machine*
*scraps of tinsel fabric*
*wadding (batting)*
*dressmaker's pins*
*interfacing*
*dressmaker's scissors*
*needle and thread*
*pearl and glass beads*

### PREPARATION
Transfer the jewel designs on to scraps of water soluble fabric using the marker pen. Check your sewing machine manual for instructions on setting the machine for machine embroidery.

### 1
Stretch the water soluble fabric over the hoop. With the thick metallic thread in the bobbin, and fine metallic thread in the machine, stitch the outline. Fill in the shape with stitches, omitting the setting holes. Make one large and several small pieces.

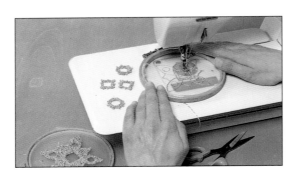

### 2
Dissolve the water soluble fabric and leave the embroidery to dry. Place a scrap of tinsel fabric behind the embroidery. Push the wadding (batting) into the setting holes until the tinsel fabric projects through. Pin on a piece of interfacing, to hold it in place.

### 3
Machine round the wadding and cut away any excess fabric. Hand stitch pearl and glass beads round the edge of the setting. Decorate to your own taste.

### 4
Finally, slip-stitch the jewels to the top and brim of the hat.

# TEMPLATES

· · · · · ·

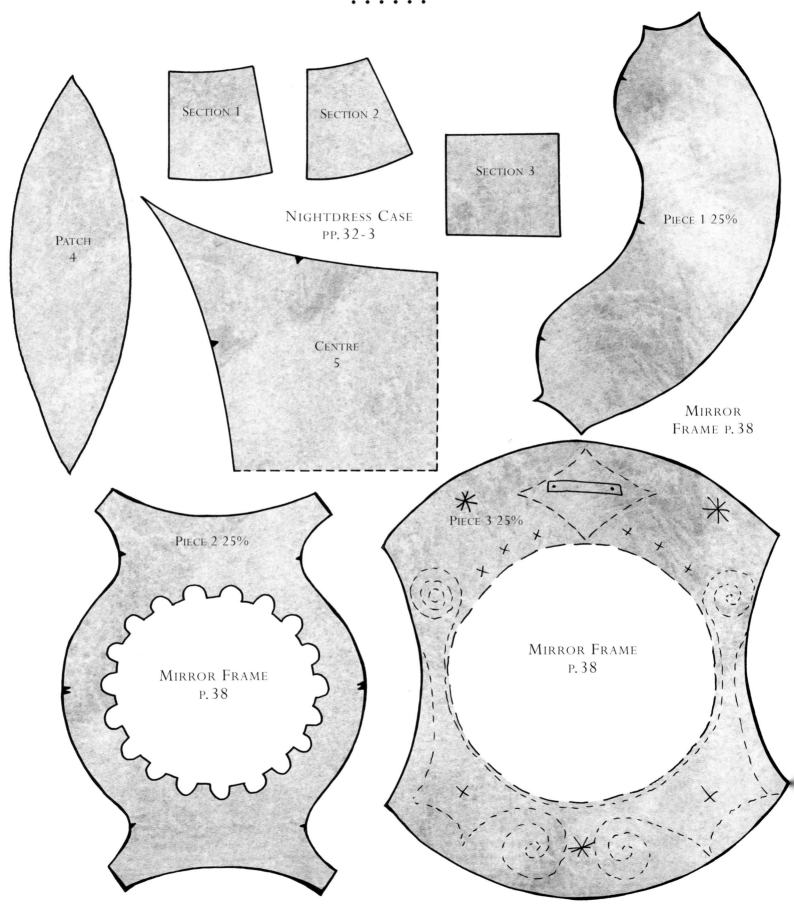

SECTION 1

SECTION 2

SECTION 3

NIGHTDRESS CASE
PP. 32-3

PATCH
4

CENTRE
5

PIECE 1 25%

MIRROR
FRAME P. 38

PIECE 2 25%

MIRROR FRAME
P. 38

PIECE 3 25%

MIRROR FRAME
P. 38

MEDIEVAL QUILT PP.40-41
MOTIFS 50%

MEDIEVAL QUILT
PP. 40-41
MOTIFS 50%

QUILTED
WAISTCOAT P. 42
33⅓ %

QUILTED HAT
PP. 46-7

PIECE 3
25%

PIECE 1
25%

QUILTED HAT
PP. 46-7

PIECE 2
25%

BAG 50%

HANDLE 50%

SIDE PIECE
50%

SATIN HANDBAG
PP. 56-7

BRODERIE PERSE
APPLIQUÉ NAPKINS
P. 51

# INDEX
. . . . . .

# ACKNOWLEDGEMENTS
. . . . . .

The Publishers would like to thank the following craftspeople who designed and made the projects for this book: Louise Brownlow, Rachel Frost, Rachel Hyde, Judith Izatt, Karen Spurgin, Karen Triffitt and Dorothy Wood. With special thanks to Isabel Stanley for her input in commissioning work and designing and making many of the projects herself. With thanks to Kay Dimbleby and her clients for permission to photograph the quilt on page 7 b. Additional photography by John Freeman, page 7 b, and Steve Tanner, pages 6 and 7 t.